MYSTICAL GIRL

MYSTICAL GIRL

Your Cosmic Journey To Self-Discovery

K. L. Carter

"Look again at that dot. That's here. That's home. That's us. On it, everyone you love, everyone you know, everyone you ever heard of, every human being who ever was, lived out their lives."

— Carl Sagan, Pale Blue Dot

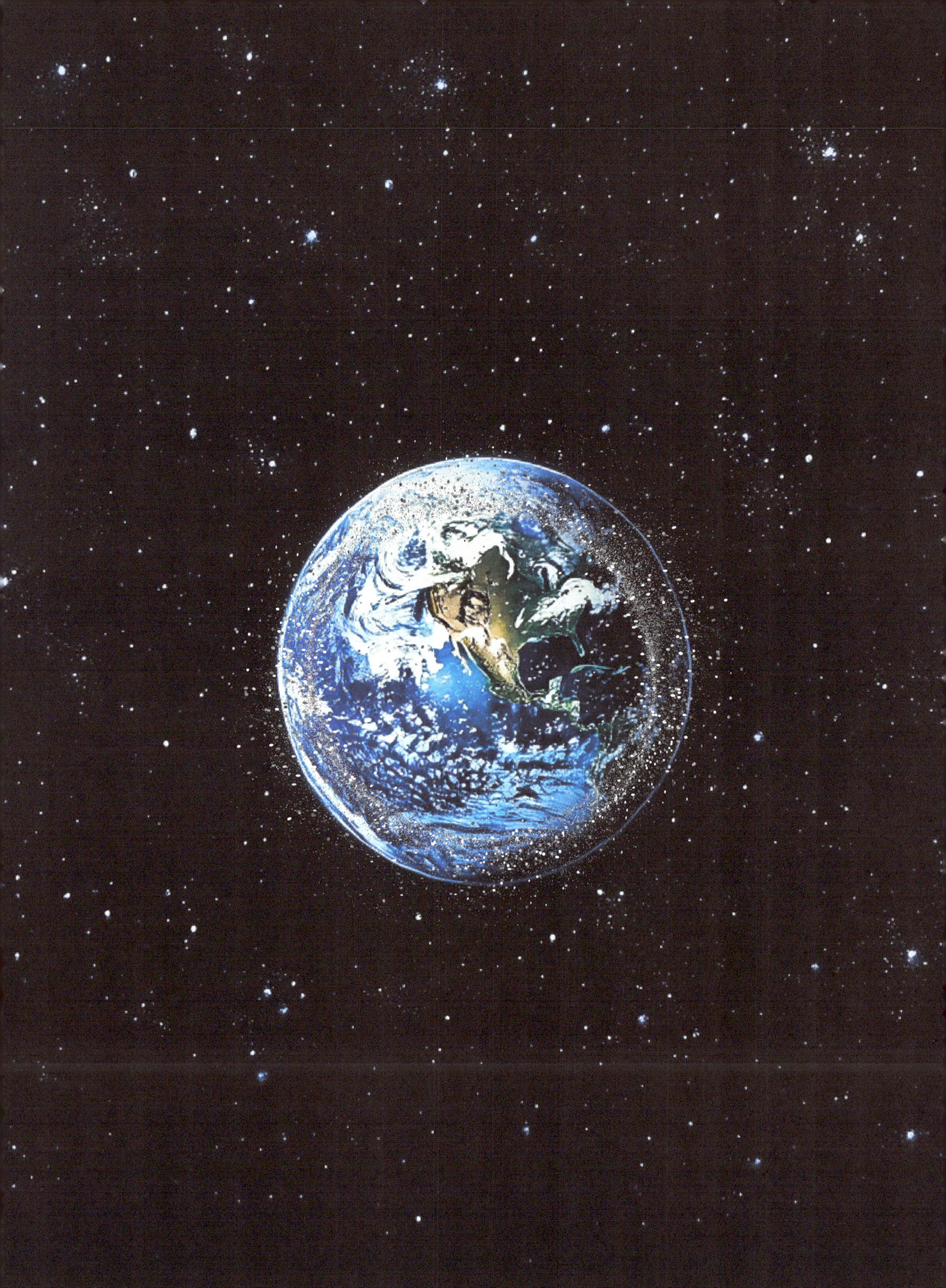

This is a work of fiction. Names, characters, places, events, and incidents are either the product of the author's imagination or used fictitiously. Any resemblance to actual persons, living or dead, or real events is purely coincidental.

Library of Congress Cataloging-in-Publication Data has been applied for.

Published by K. L. Carter
Lancaster, California, United States of America
ISBN: 979-8-9922780-2-6

Printed in the United States of America
First Edition: 2024

Cover Design: K. L. Carter

Image Credits:
Images in this book were created using AI-generated tools from MidJourney. The author holds commercial rights to these images under MidJourney's paid subscription licensing terms.

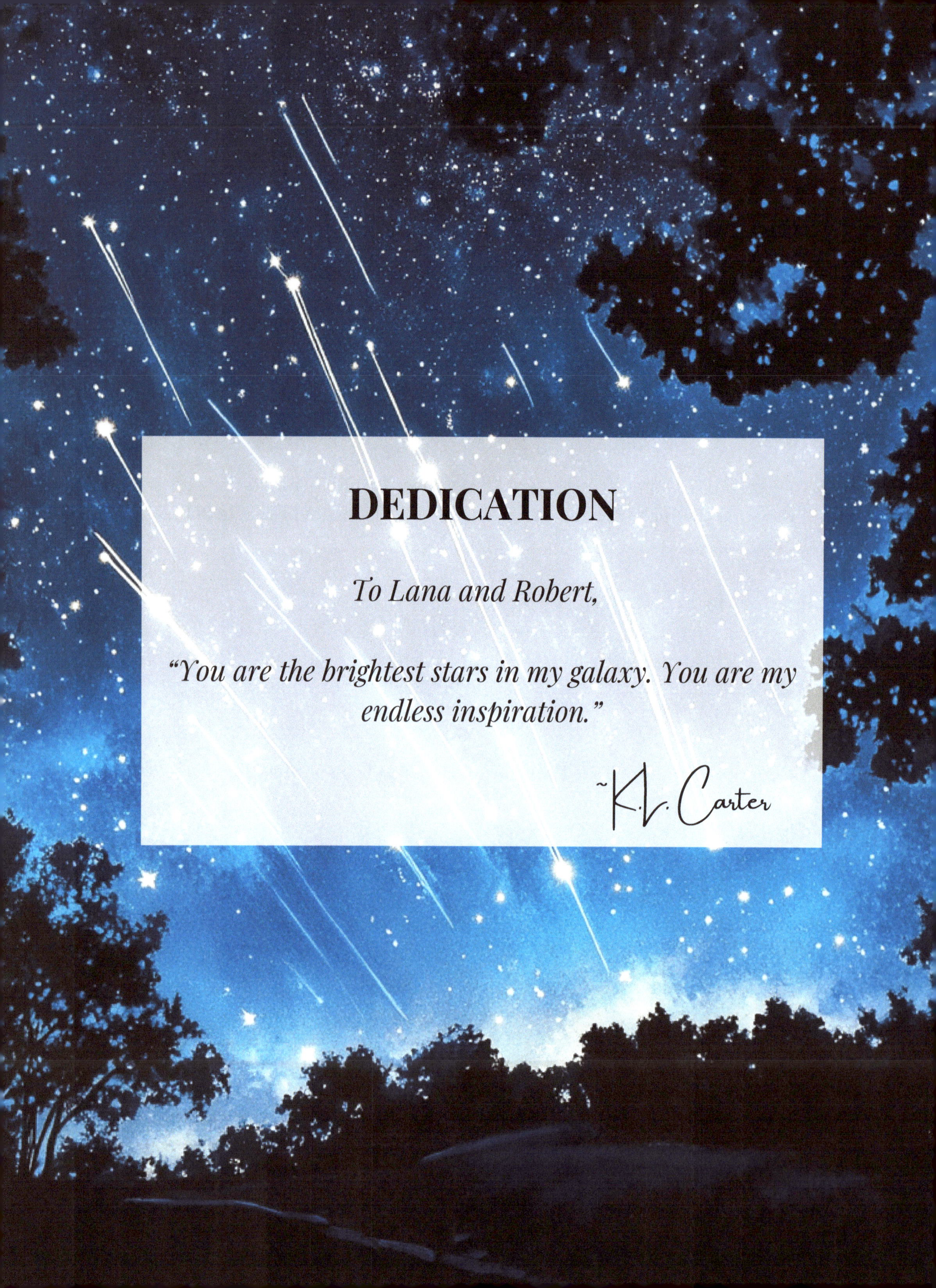

DEDICATION

To Lana and Robert,

"You are the brightest stars in my galaxy. You are my endless inspiration."

~K.L. Carter

ACKNOWLEDGEMENTS

A heartfelt thank-you to my mentors, mentees, family, friends, colleagues, and all those who inspire me.

~K.L. Carter

Table of Contents

Introduction
A Cosmic Invitation

"The cosmos calls not to be conquered, but to be felt—
a reminder that the greatest universe to explore is the one within."
— K.L. Carter

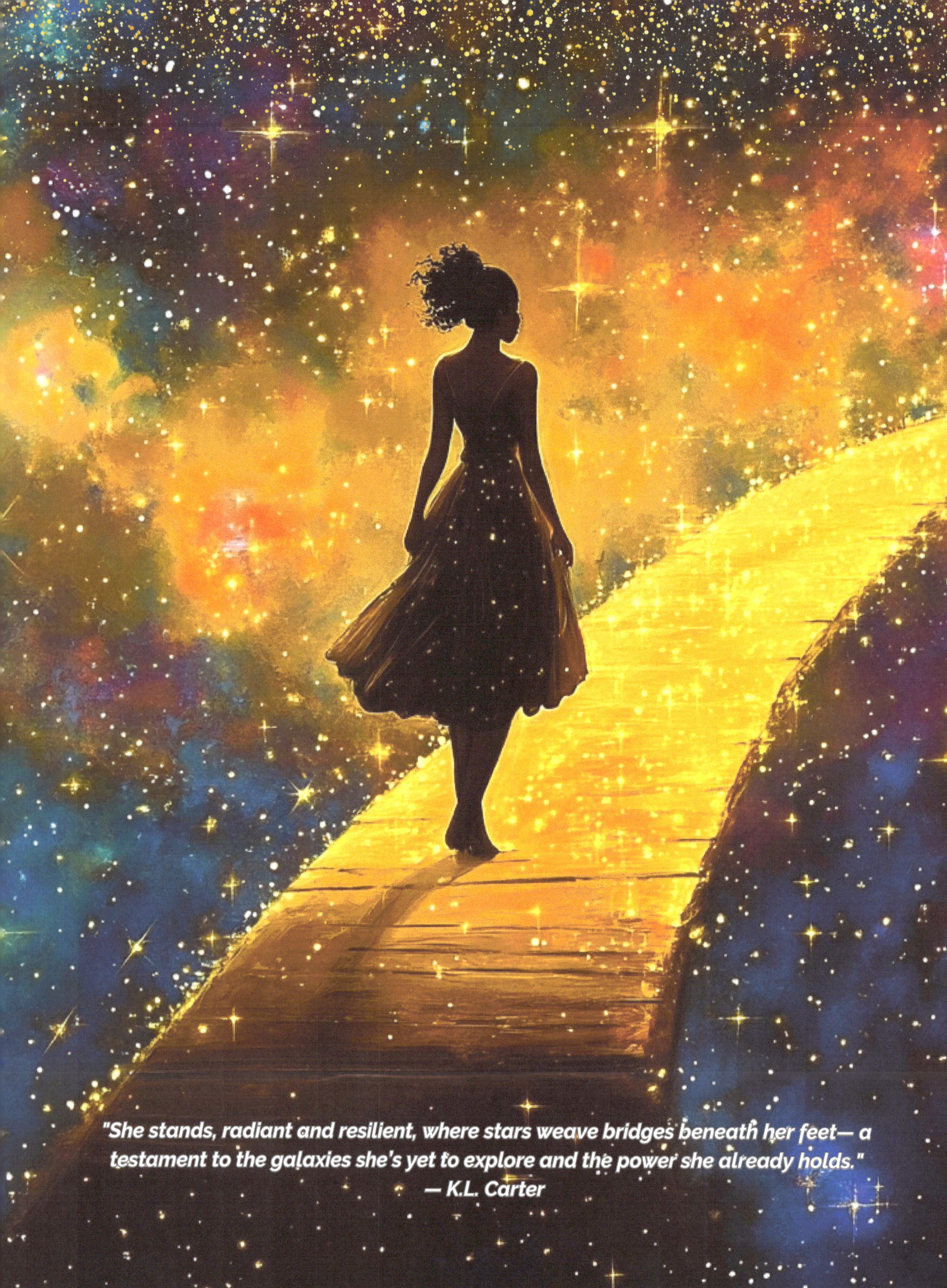
"She stands, radiant and resilient, where stars weave bridges beneath her feet— a testament to the galaxies she's yet to explore and the power she already holds."
— K.L. Carter

Introduction
Welcome, Mystical Girl

"You are a galaxy wrapped in human form, a constellation of dreams, a star chart of endless possibilities."
— K.L. Carter

There's a part of you that no telescope can find, no probe can touch, no satellite can scan. A space within you more expansive than the Milky Way, where your soul charts its own constellations. You are a universe of dreams, wonder, and whimsy — an explorer of the intangible, the mystical, the extraordinary you.

This is your cosmic journey—a deeply personal exploration of the intangible you. It's not about finding answers but about embracing the questions, the wonder, and the magic of simply being.

Together, we'll zoom out, twirl through galaxies of thought, and discover what makes you uniquely, magnificently you.

So buckle up, *Mystical Girl*. This is your cosmic journey, your personal exploration of the intangible self. No boarding passes needed, just an open mind, a curious heart, and the courage to leap into the unknown.

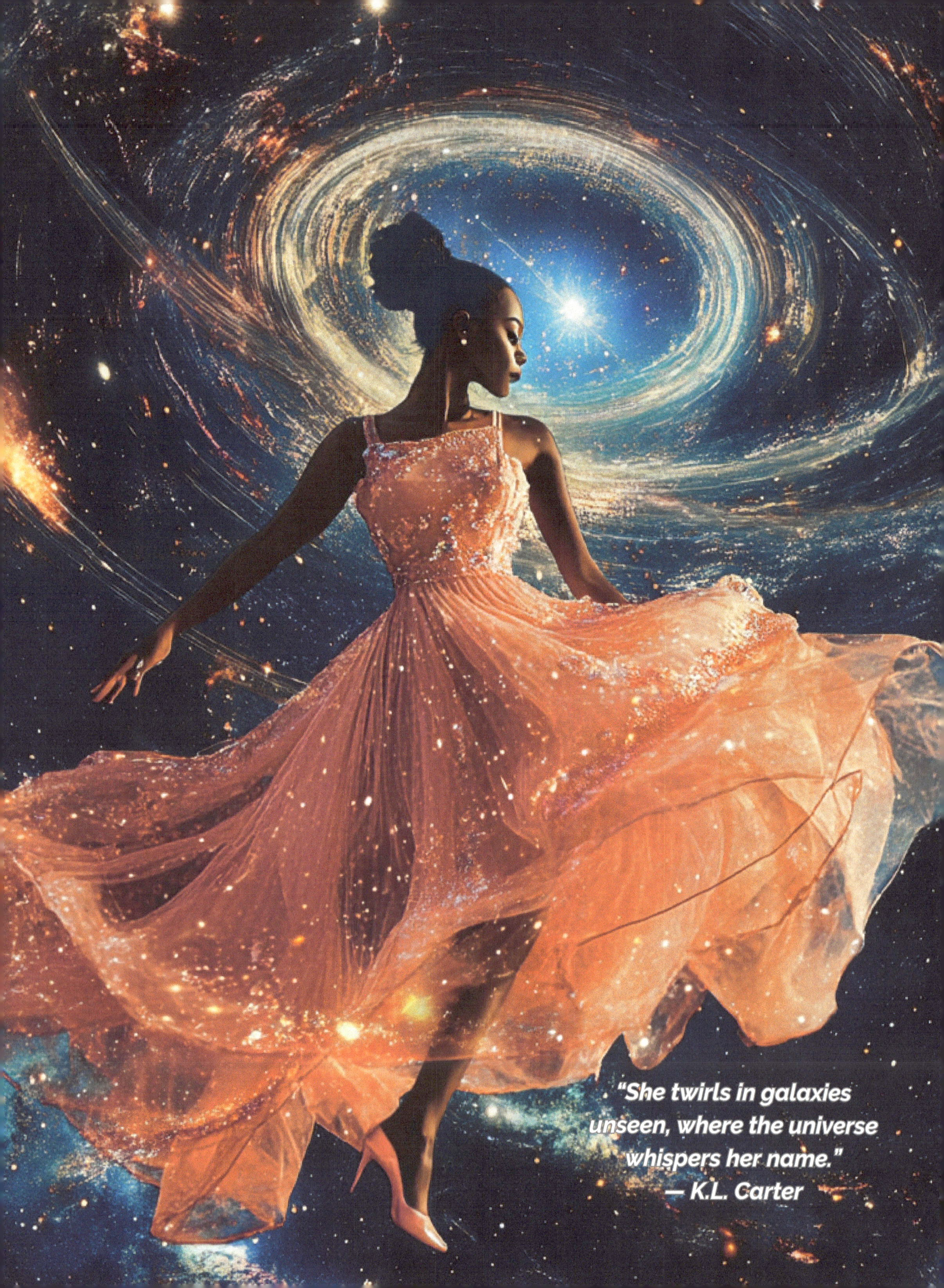
"She twirls in galaxies unseen, where the universe whispers her name."
— K.L. Carter

Chapter 1
Launch Pad: Stardust and Soulprints

"She twirls in galaxies unseen, where the universe whispers her name."
— K.L. Carter

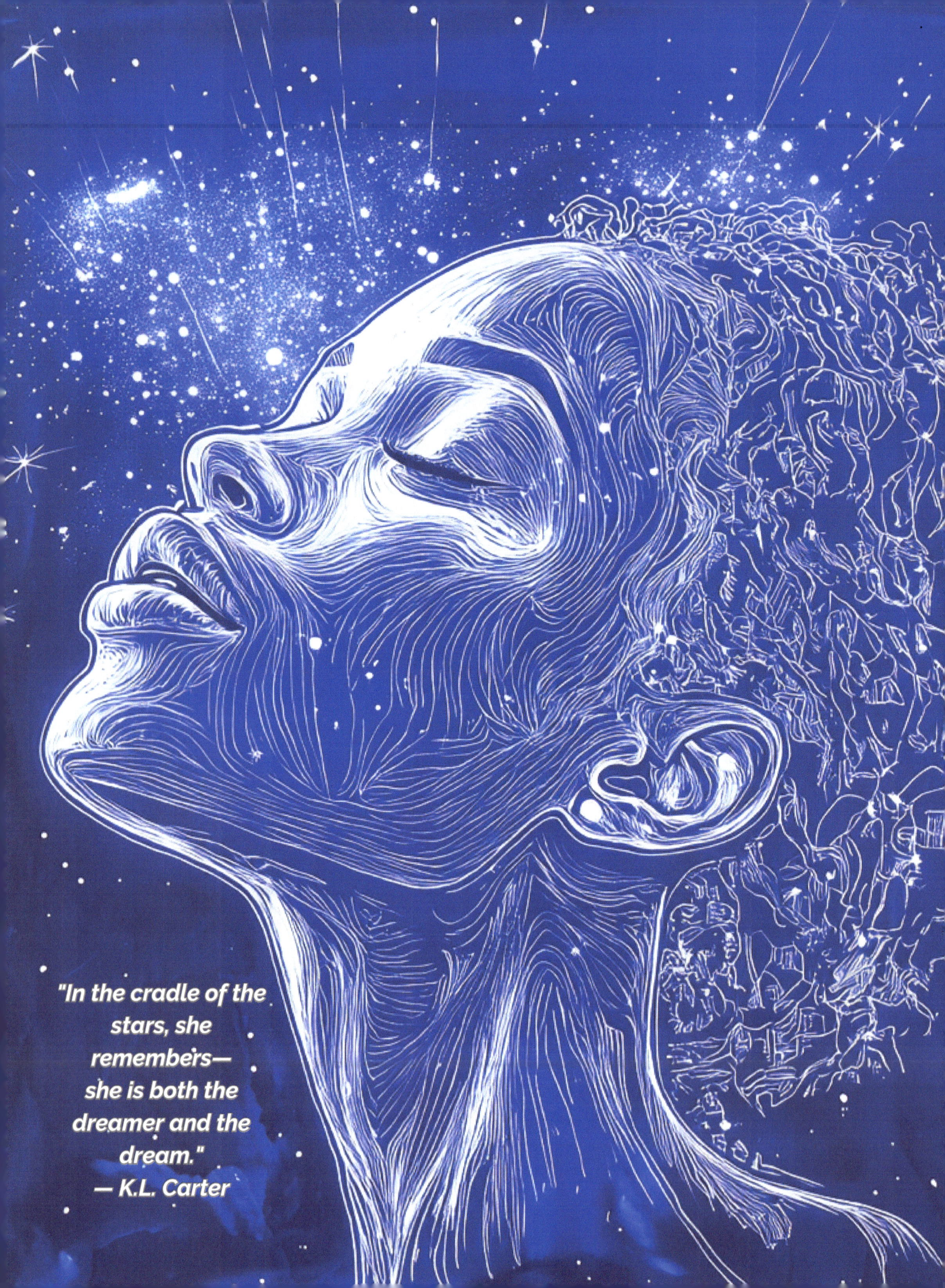
"In the cradle of the stars, she remembers— she is both the dreamer and the dream."
— K.L. Carter

Chapter 1
Launch Pad: Stardust and Soulprints

"You are a galaxy wrapped in human form, a constellation of dreams, a star chart of endless possibilities."
— K.L. Carter

Mystical Girl, did you know you're made of stardust? Literally. The iron in your blood, the calcium in your bones, the very oxygen you breathe all came from stars that exploded billions of years ago.

And just like the stars, you carry within you the essence of creation. Every thought, every emotion, every dream leaves a soulprint — an intangible map of who you are and who you're becoming.

"Empowered women empower women. And your journey to self-discovery doesn't just elevate you — it inspires those around you to shine brighter too."

Ask yourself:

- What lights you up?
- What constellations have you drawn from the chaos of your experiences?
- Where does your soul want to travel next?

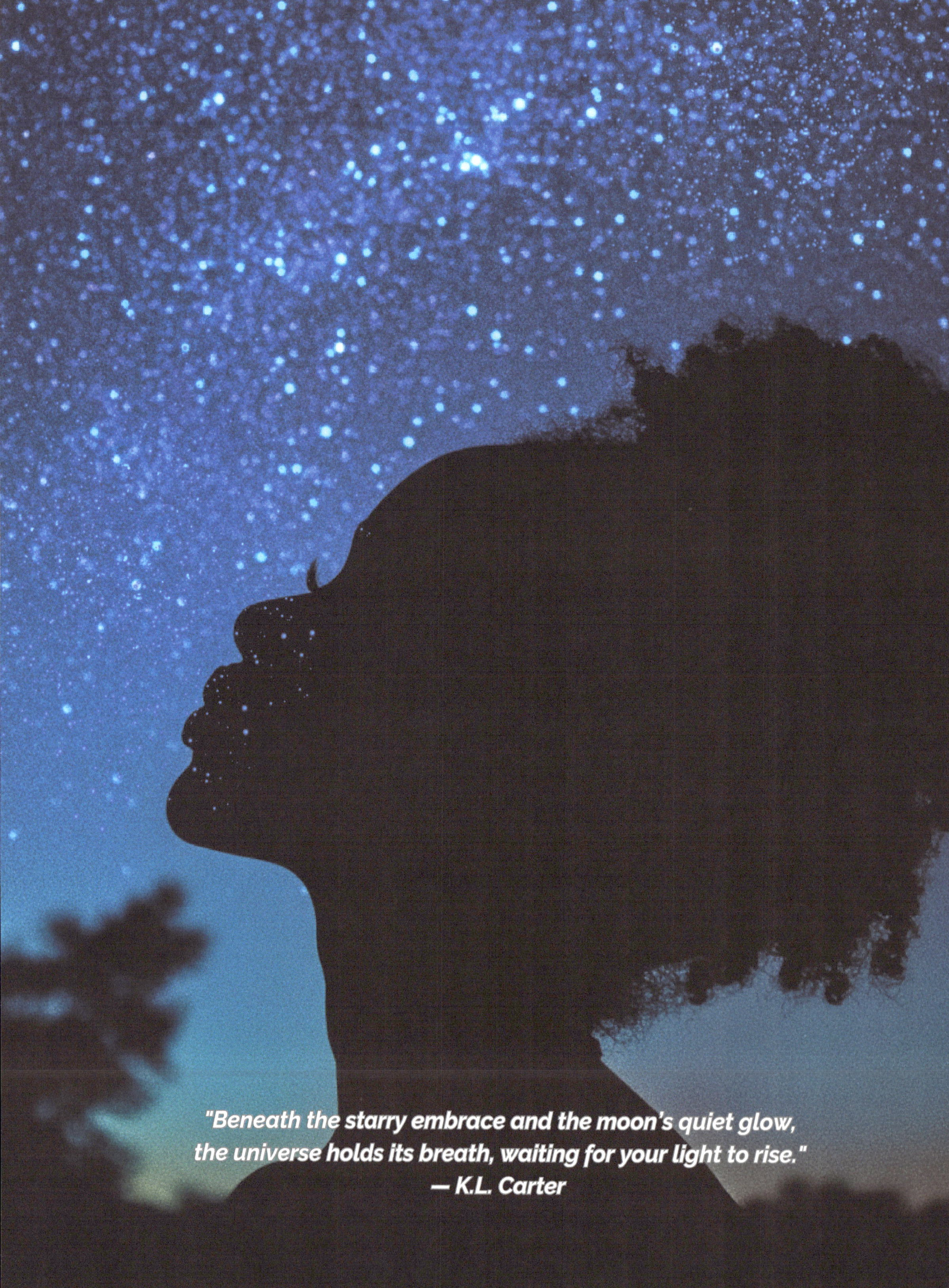
"Beneath the starry embrace and the moon's quiet glow,
the universe holds its breath, waiting for your light to rise."
— K.L. Carter

Chapter 2
Warp Speed: Chasing the Intangible

"The intangible you is not seen in the mirror but felt in the glow of your kindness, the spark of your dreams, and the strength of your soul."
— K.L. Carter

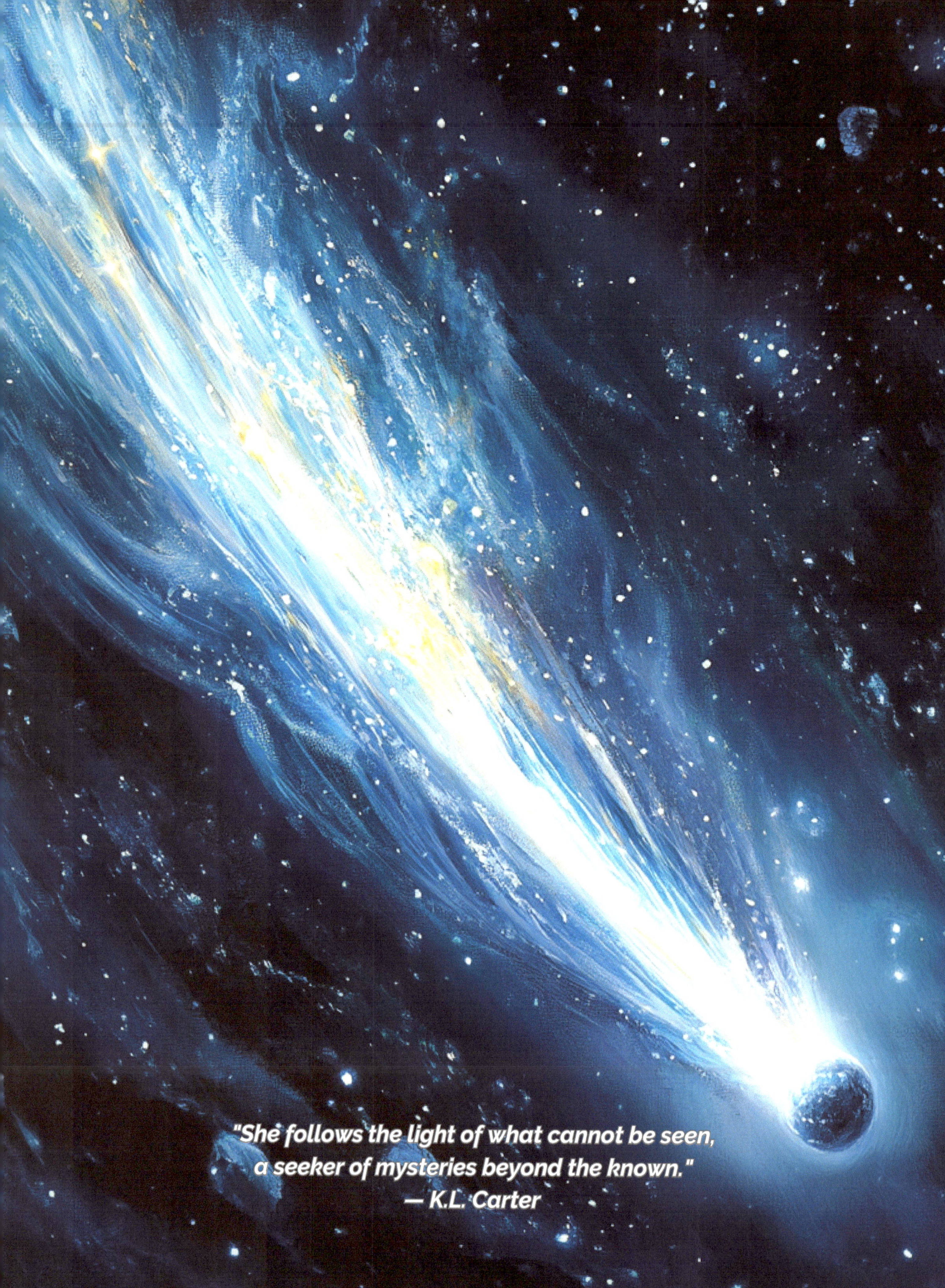
"She follows the light of what cannot be seen,
a seeker of mysteries beyond the known."
— K.L. Carter

Chapter 2
Warp Speed: Chasing the Intangible

"The intangible you is a shooting star — fleeting, beautiful, impossible to grasp, yet unforgettable."
— K.L. Carter

The intangible you isn't found in the physical — your job title, your possessions, or even your reflection in the mirror. It's found in the glow of your laughter, the warmth of your kindness, the quiet strength of your resilience.

To explore this space, you must embrace the whimsical. Dare to believe in the impossible. Imagine your soul as a spaceship, gliding through galaxies of thought, emotion, and creativity.

- What makes your heart race like a comet streaking through the night?
- What mysteries do you long to unravel in the quiet corners of your mind?
- What cosmic adventures are waiting for you to take the first step?

"Zoom out, breathe in, and let the stars remind you of your strength."
— K.L. Carter

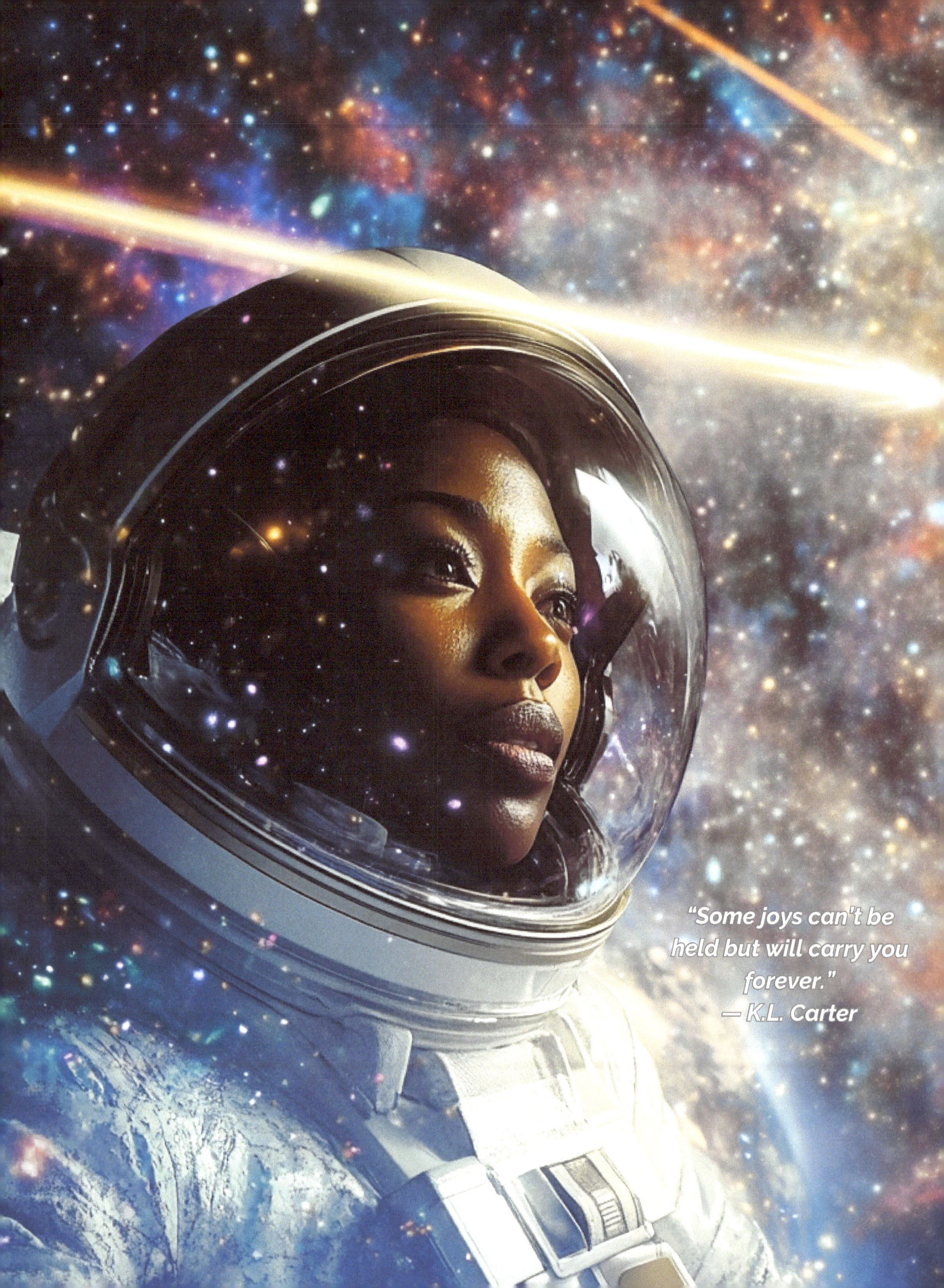
"Some joys can't be
held but will carry you
forever."
— K.L. Carter

Chapter 3
Nebula Whimsy: The Art of Being You

"Her soul, a nebula of dreams,
weaves starlight into the fabric of her reality."
— K.L. Carter

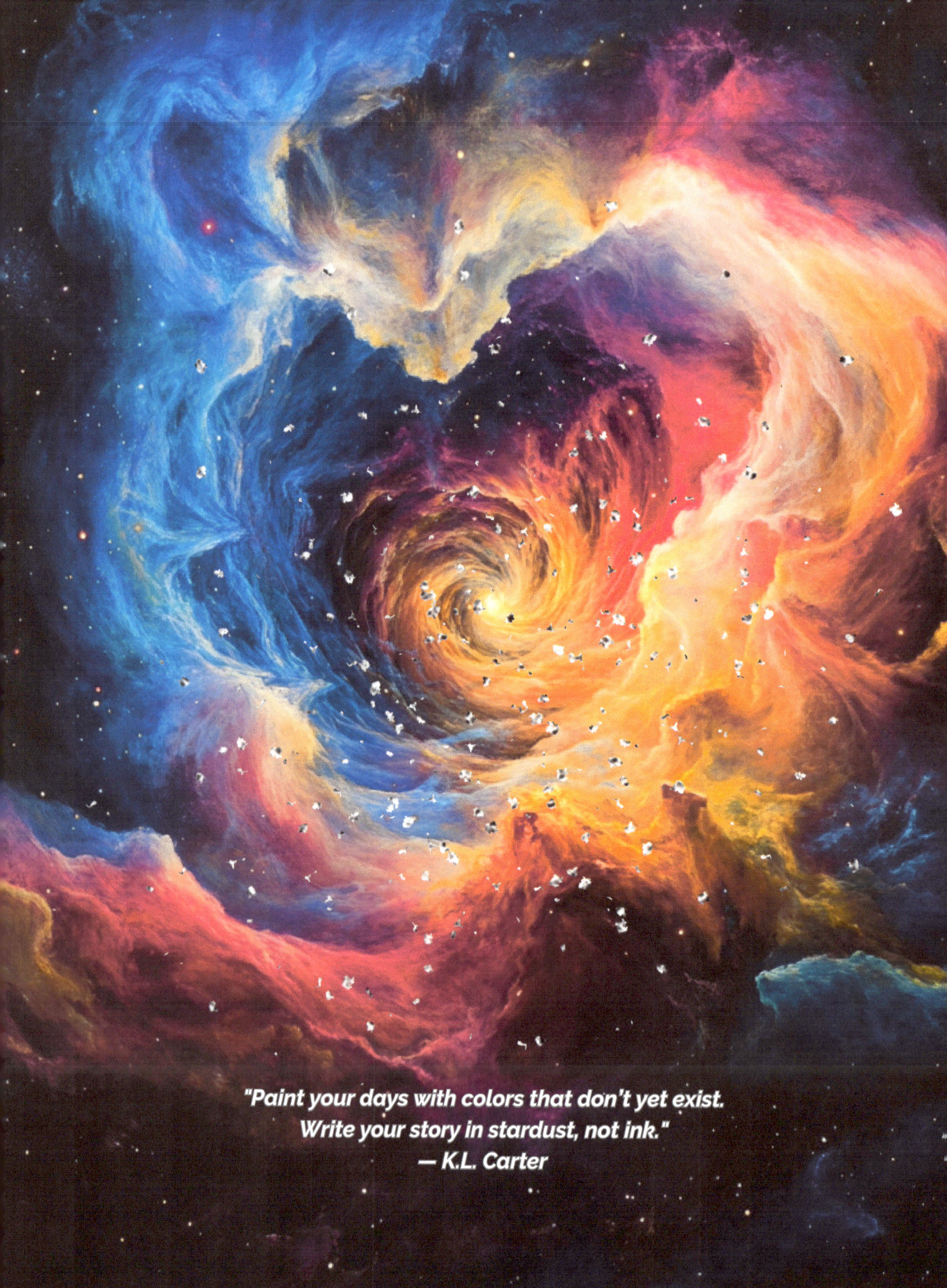
"Paint your days with colors that don't yet exist.
Write your story in stardust, not ink."
— K.L. Carter

Chapter 3
Nebula Whimsy: The Art of Being You

"Mystical Girl, you're not just exploring space — you're creating it. Like a nebula birthing stars, you have the power to craft your own universe."
— K.L. Carter

"Her soul, a nebula of dreams, weaves starlight into reality."

- Paint your days with colors that don't yet exist.
- Write your story in stardust, not ink.
- Dance in the gravity of your own joy, spinning like a planet that refuses to stop.

And don't forget to twirl. Yes, twirl! Spin yourself into the galaxies of possibility, with your head thrown back and your heart wide open.

"She twirls in galaxies unseen, where the universe whispers her name."
— K.L. Carter

You are not meant to be caught — you are meant to be lived.

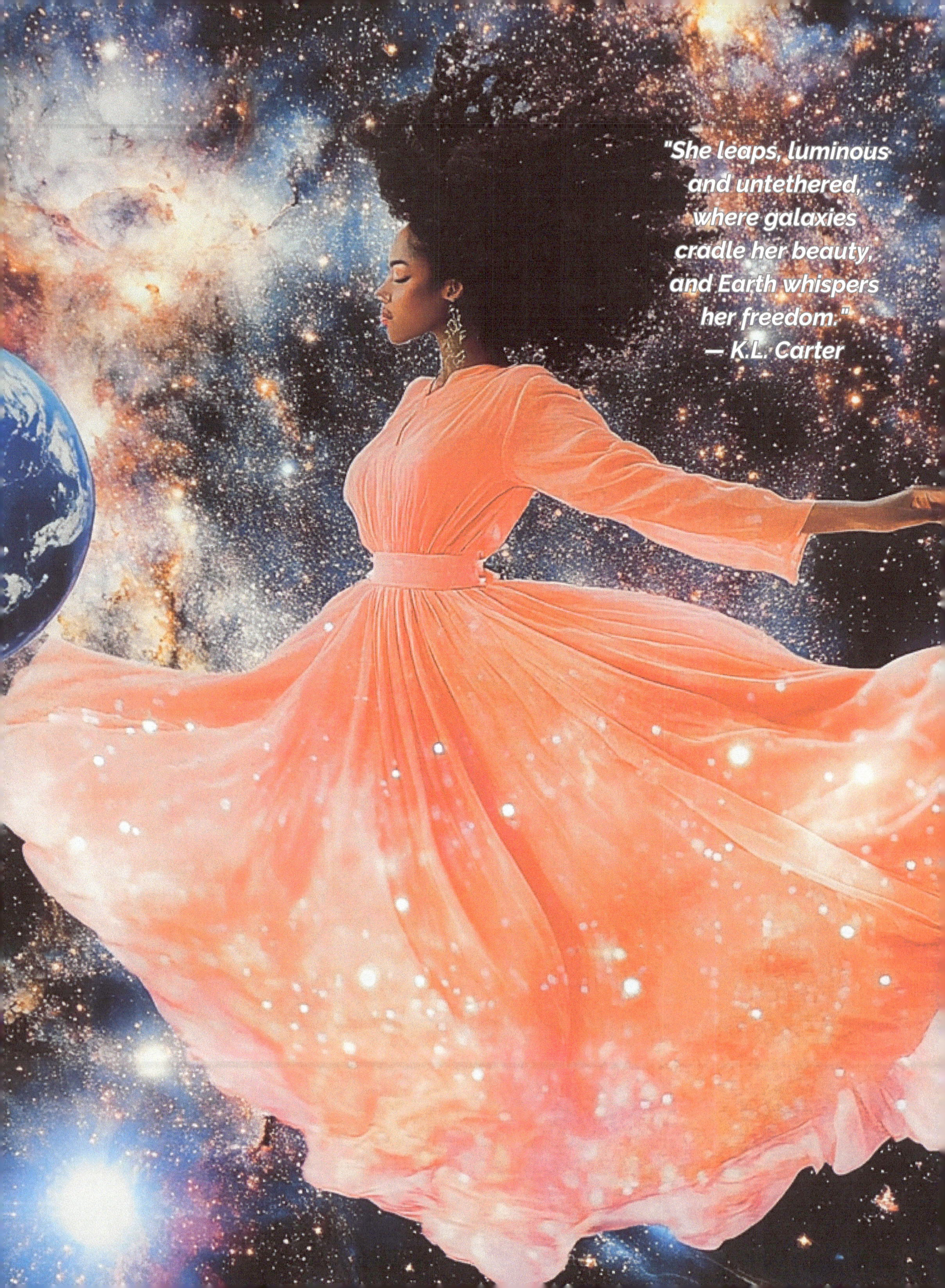
"She leaps, luminous
and untethered,
where galaxies
cradle her beauty,
and Earth whispers
her freedom."
— K.L. Carter

Chapter 4
Intergalactic Checkpoints: Reflections for the Soul

"From the heavens above, she sees—
the power of perspective transforms everything."
— K.L. Carter

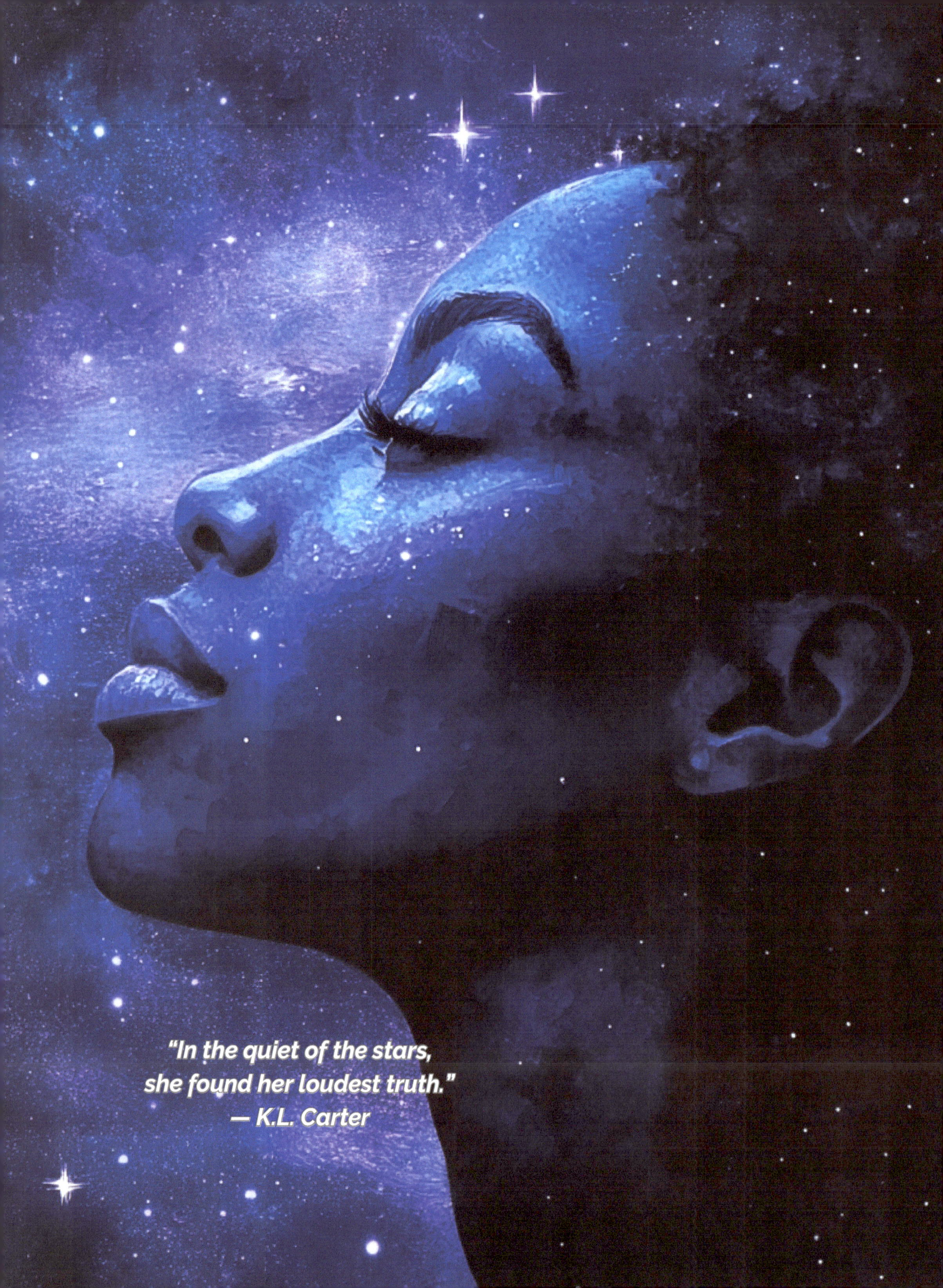
"In the quiet of the stars,
she found her loudest truth."
— K.L. Carter

Chapter 4
Intergalactic Checkpoints: Reflections for the Soul

"Mystical Girl, in the quiet of your soul, you gather starlight—
not as fragments, but as luminous truths, guiding you toward the joy of who you're becoming."
— K.L. Carter

As you travel through the cosmos of your own being, take moments to pause and reflect:

- What have I discovered about myself today?
- What have I created in the vastness of my inner space?
- How can I align my earthly actions with my cosmic dreams?

"In the quiet of the stars, she found her loudest truth."
— K.L. Carter

These checkpoints aren't meant to anchor you — they're meant to propel you forward.

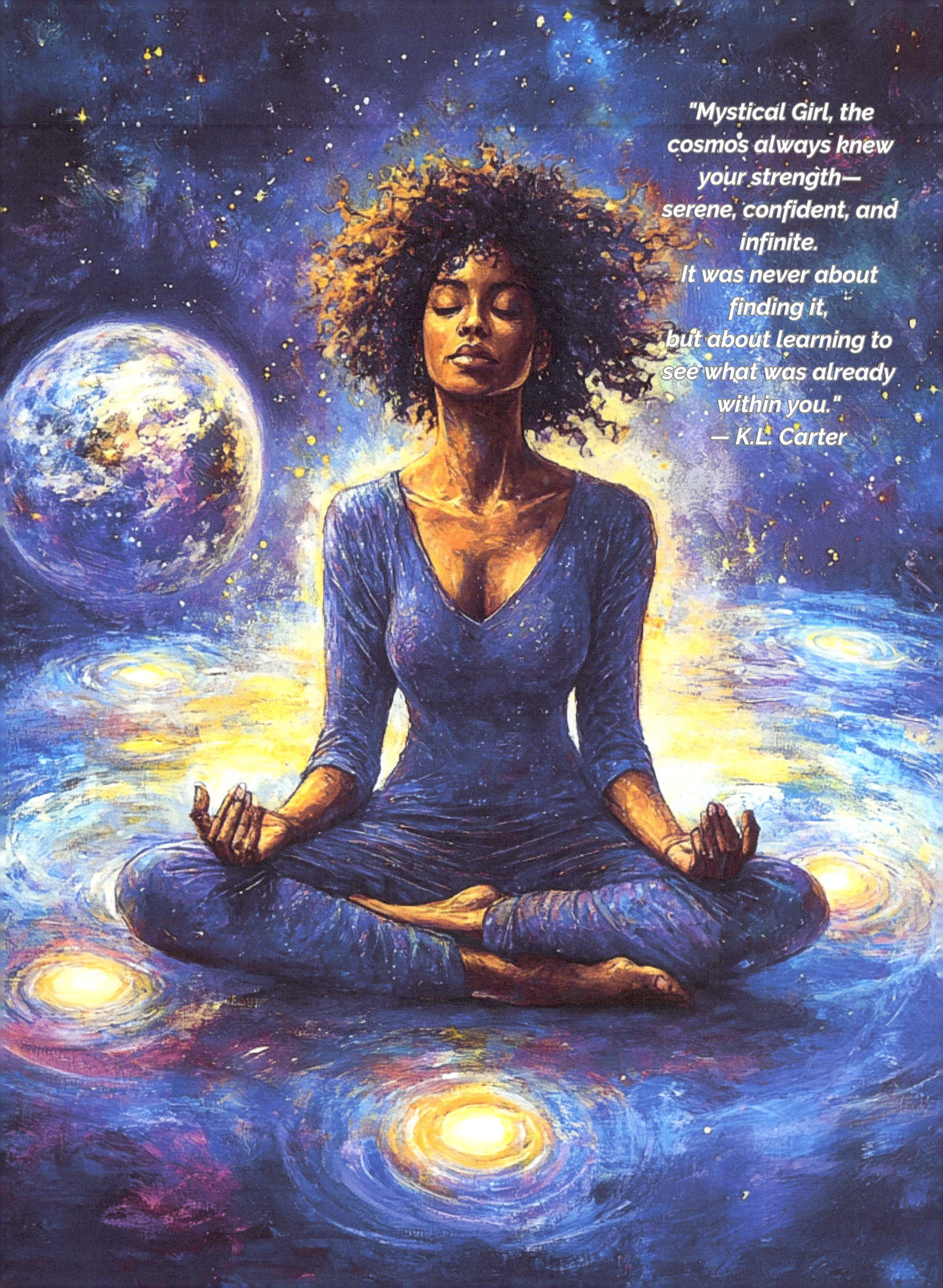
"Mystical Girl, the
cosmos always knew
your strength—
serene, confident, and
infinite.
It was never about
finding it,
but about learning to
see what was already
within you."
— K.L. Carter

Final Orbit
Your Cosmic Self

"Your cosmic self is not bound by gravity, but lifted by the infinite wonder of who you are and all you can become."
— K.L. Carter

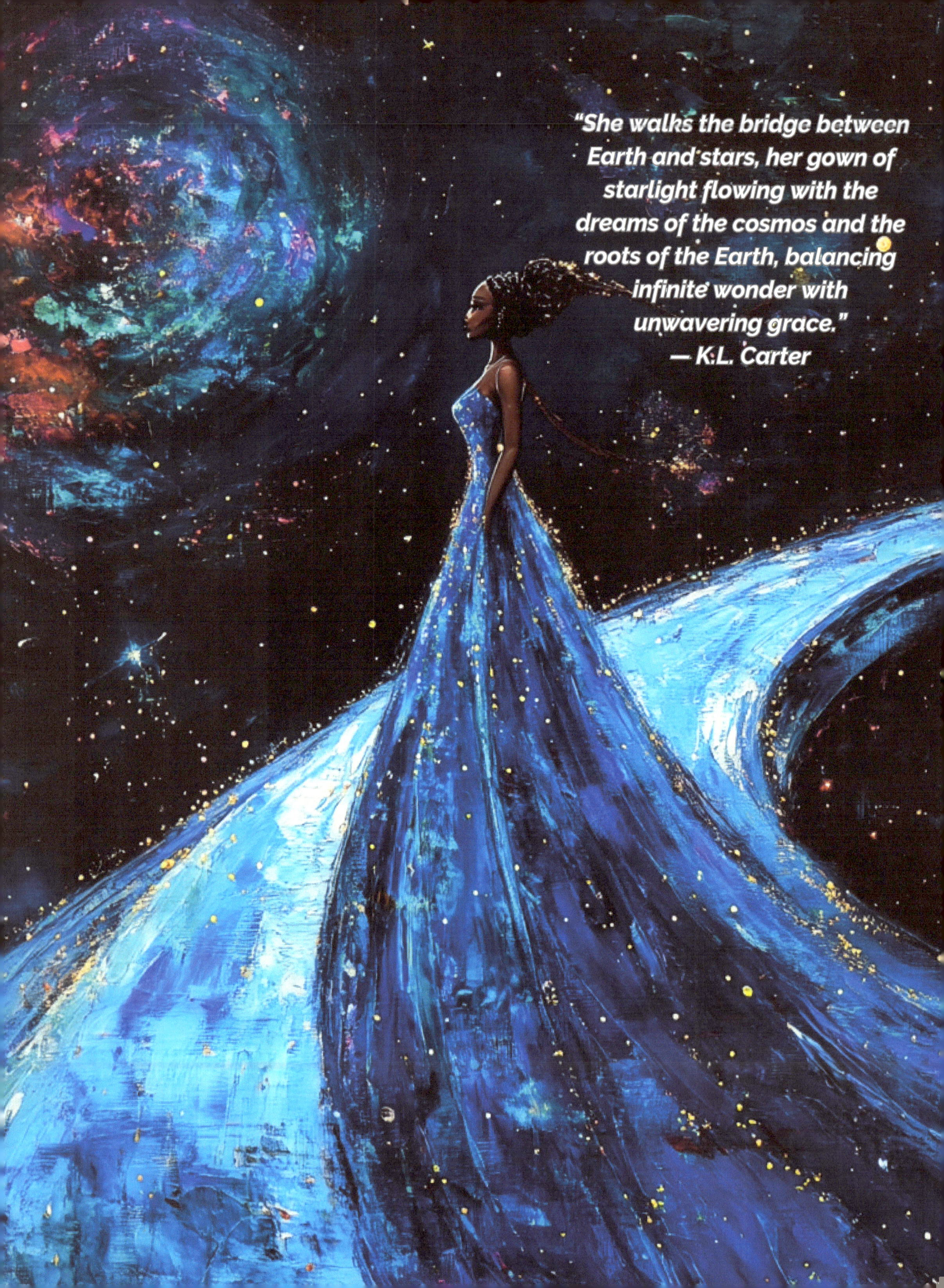
"She walks the bridge between
Earth and stars, her gown of
starlight flowing with the
dreams of the cosmos and the
roots of the Earth, balancing
infinite wonder with
unwavering grace."
— K.L. Carter

Final Orbit
Cosmic Self

"Amidst the cosmos of her mind, she found mindfulness as her anchor, self-awareness as her guide, joy as her fuel, and self-preservation as her shield. Against all odds, she became her own brightest star."
— K.L. Carter

Mystical Girl, the journey to the intangible you isn't about finding answers. It's about embracing the questions, the wonder, and the magic of simply being.

"You are a blessing to be blessed and a blessing to bless others. And sometimes you must remember to be a blessing to yourself."
— K.L. Carter

Empowerment comes from within. It's the ability to zoom out, to see your journey and your worth through a cosmic lens. Your light doesn't dim when you help others — it shines brighter.

So today, twirl in space. Reach for the stars within you. Let your soul take flight. And remember: the journey to the intangible you is the most mystical, magical adventure of all.

"Everything is everything, nothing is nothing, and you are all things to yourself."
— K.L. Carter

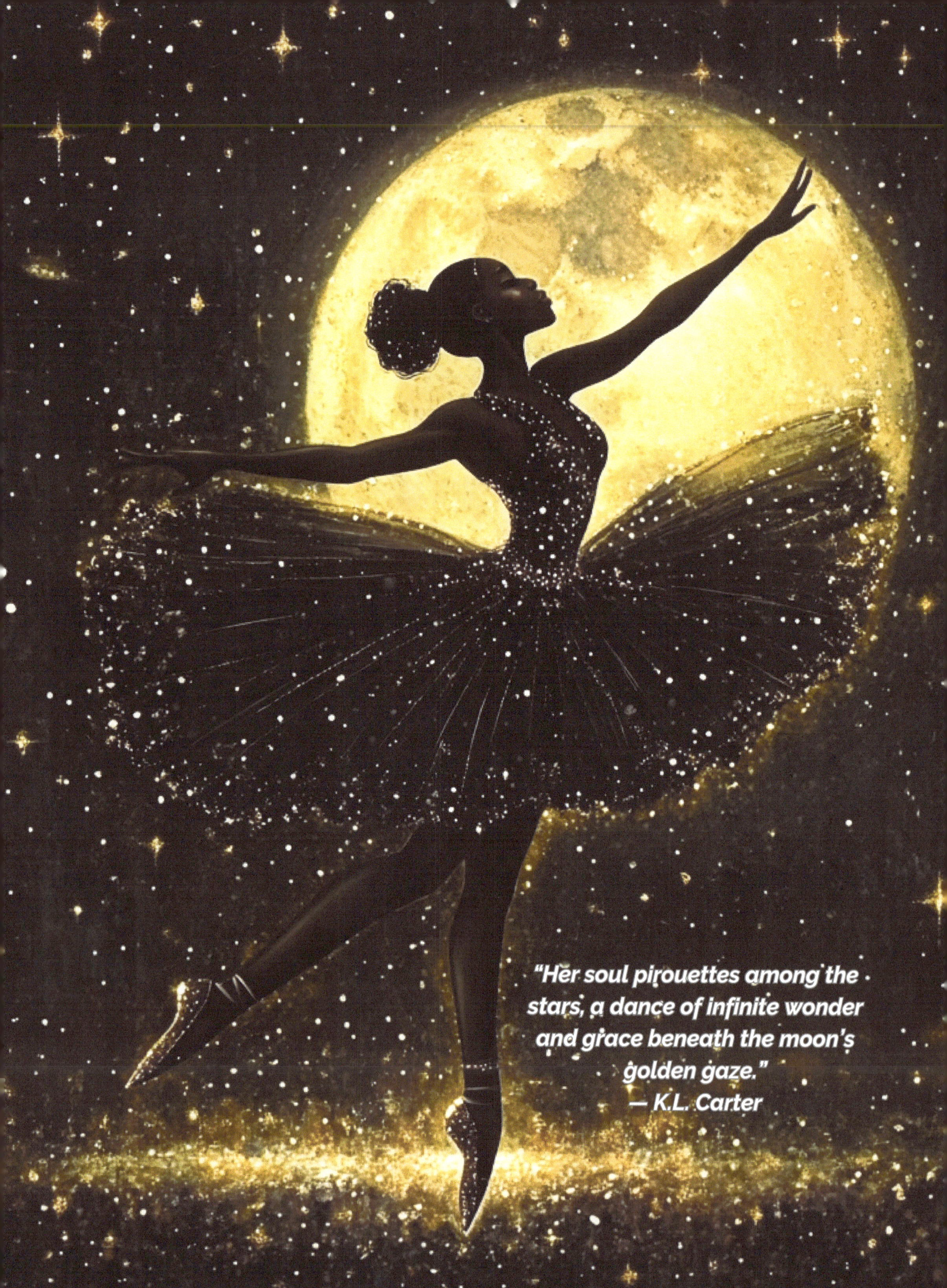
"Her soul pirouettes among the
stars, a dance of infinite wonder
and grace beneath the moon's
golden gaze."
— K.L. Carter

Mystical Girl Takeaways

Empowerment

*"The stars don't ask for permission to shine— neither should you.
Your journey is yours to claim, your light, yours to share."
— K.L. Carter*

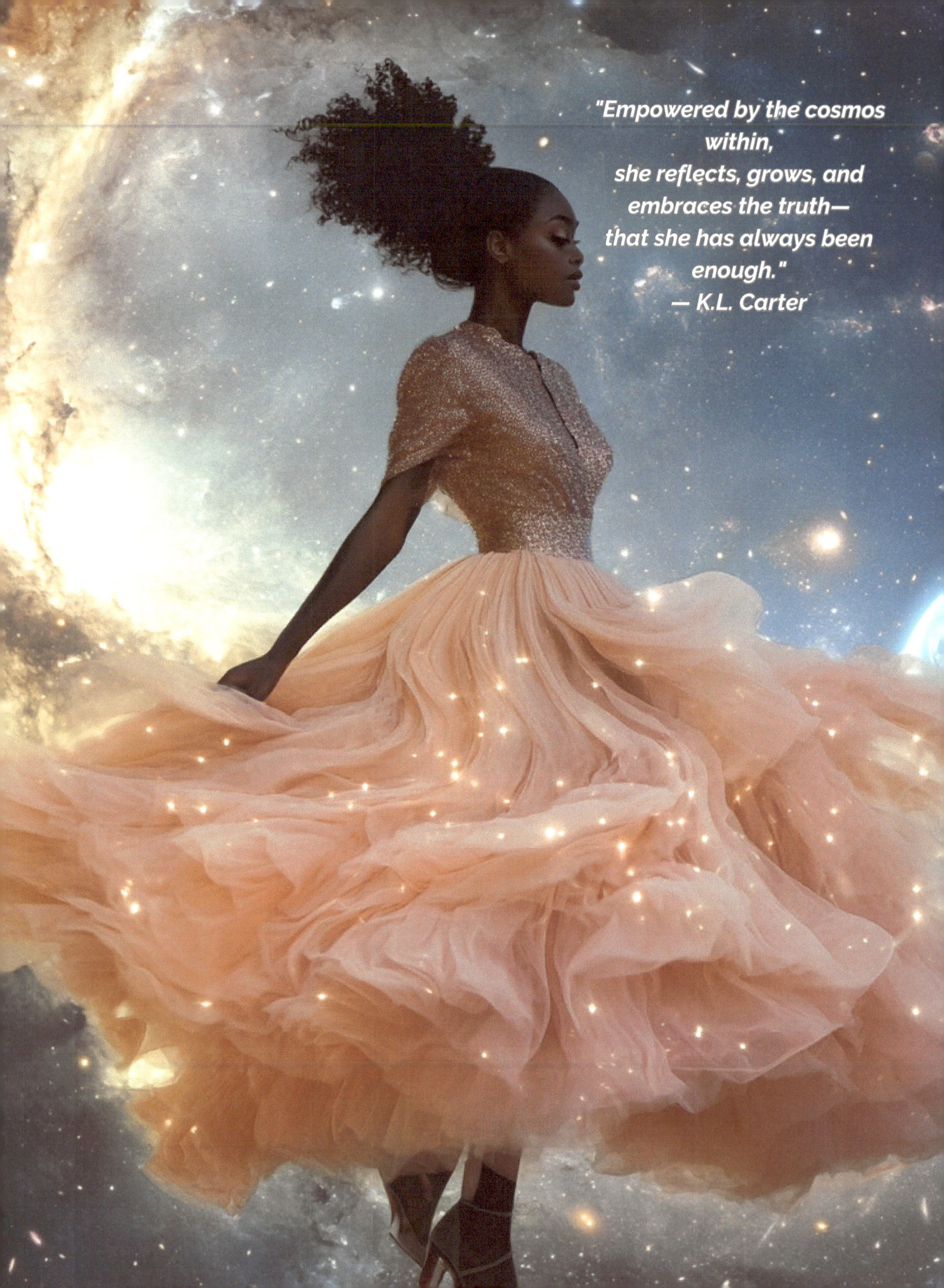
"Empowered by the cosmos within,
she reflects, grows, and embraces the truth—
that she has always been enough."
— K.L. Carter

Mystical Girl Takeaways
Empowerment

Mystical Girl Takeaways:

- **Empowered Women Empower Women**
  - Celebrate your growth and light, and share it with others. Your journey inspires those around you to take their own leaps of faith.

- **Pause and Reflect**
  - Use quiet moments to check in with yourself. What have you created? Where do you want to go next?

- **Zoom Out**
  - When life feels overwhelming, step back. Look at the bigger picture. What's stressing you out today won't define you tomorrow.

- **Celebrate Your Wins**
  - Big or small, your achievements matter. Clap for yourself — you've earned it.

- **Twirl in Your Joy**
  - Life isn't about perfection. It's about movement, exploration, and embracing the beauty of imperfection.

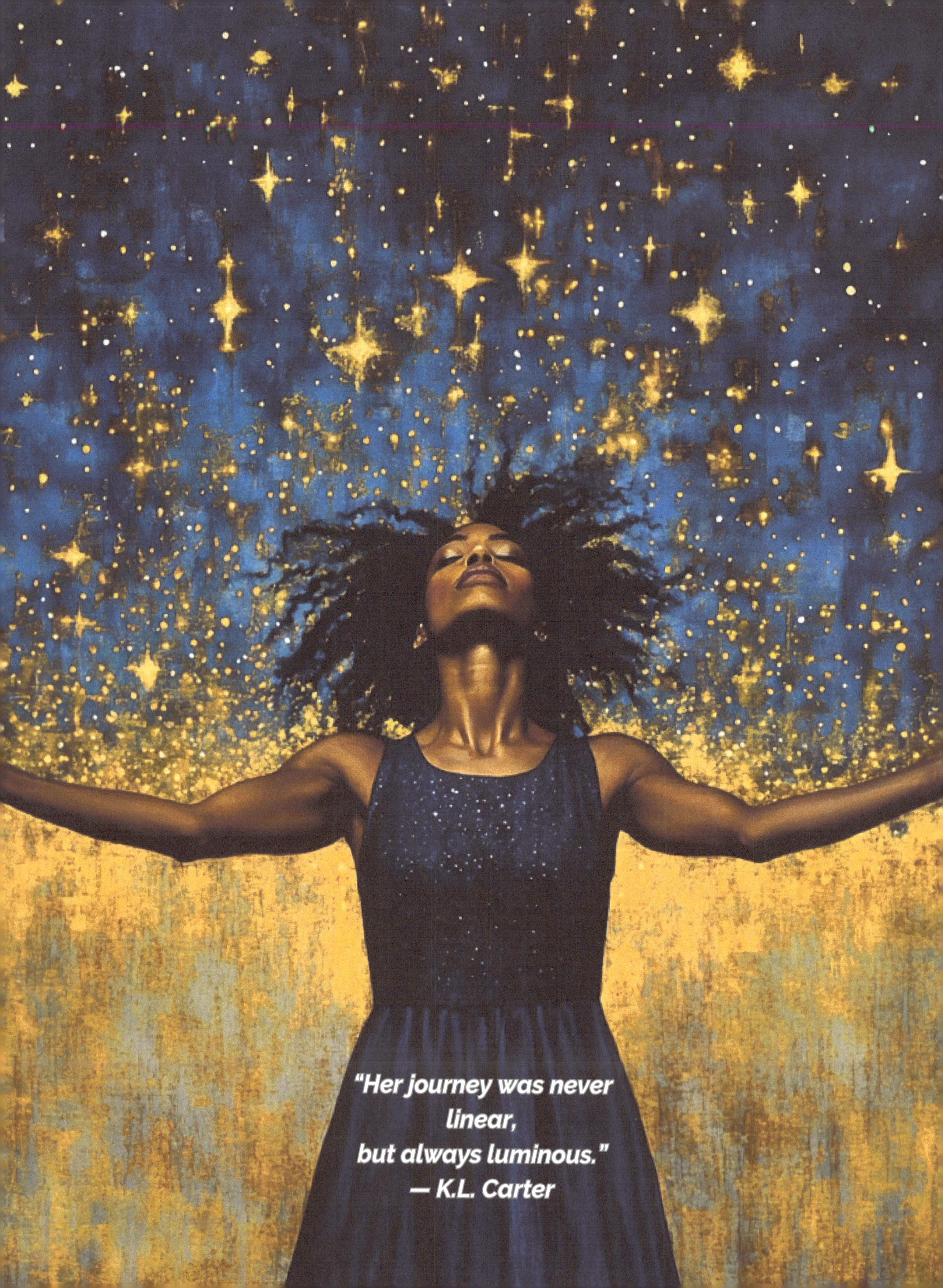
"Her journey was never
linear,
but always luminous."
— K.L. Carter

"What whispers does your soul reveal when you pause to listen?
Which stars in your journey have guided you the most?"
— K.L. Carter

Mystical Girl, as your cosmic journey continues, remember:
The answers you seek are already within you.
The stars above and the whispers within will always guide you.

Pause. Reflect. Dream.
And always, always, let your light shine.

Your journey is yours to create,
and your soul is its brightest star.

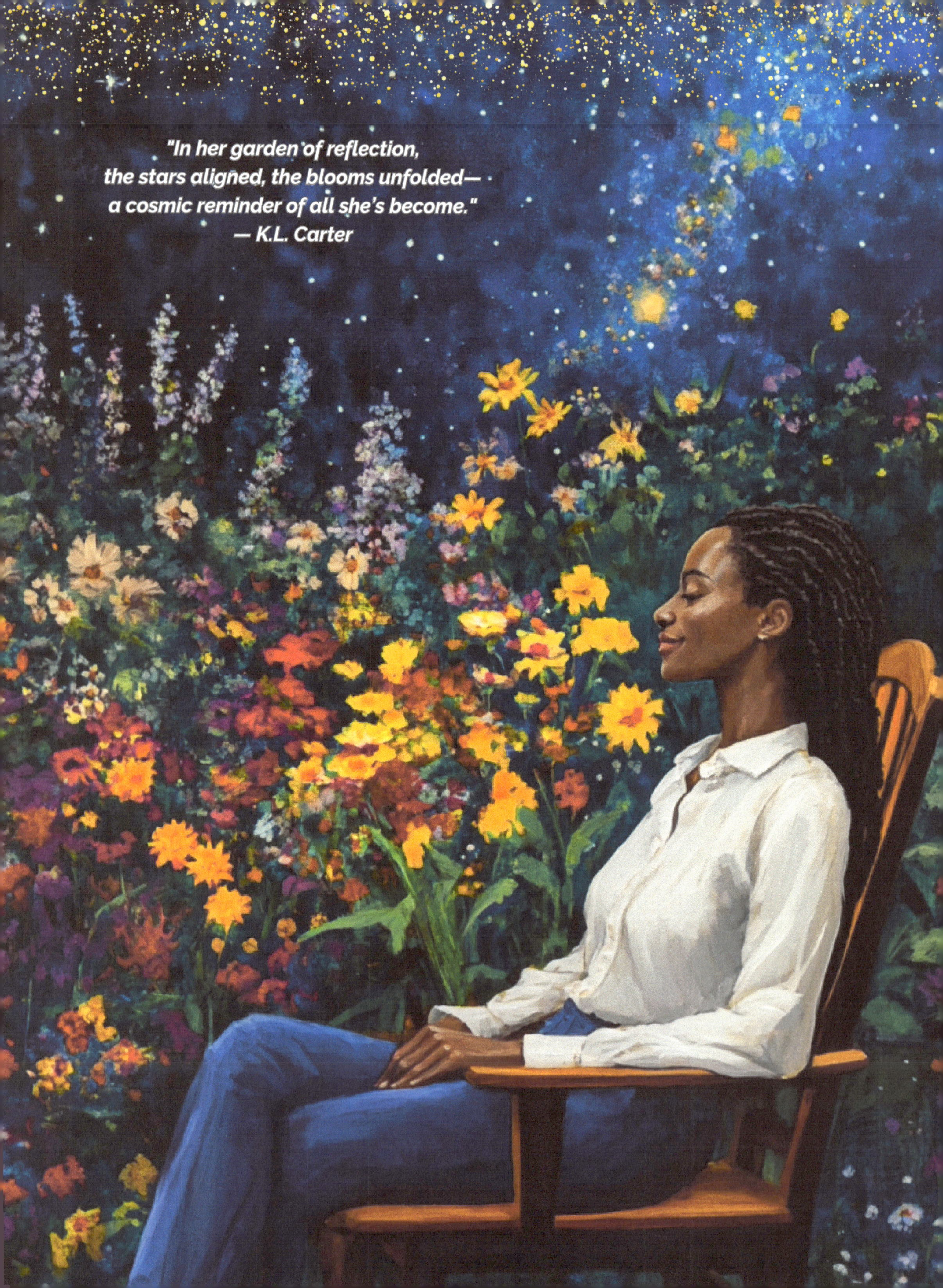
"In her garden of reflection,
the stars aligned, the blooms unfolded—
a cosmic reminder of all she's become."
— K.L. Carter

Meet the Author
K. L. Carter

"Your cosmic self is not bound by gravity, but lifted by the infinite wonder of who you are and all you can become."
— K.L. Carter

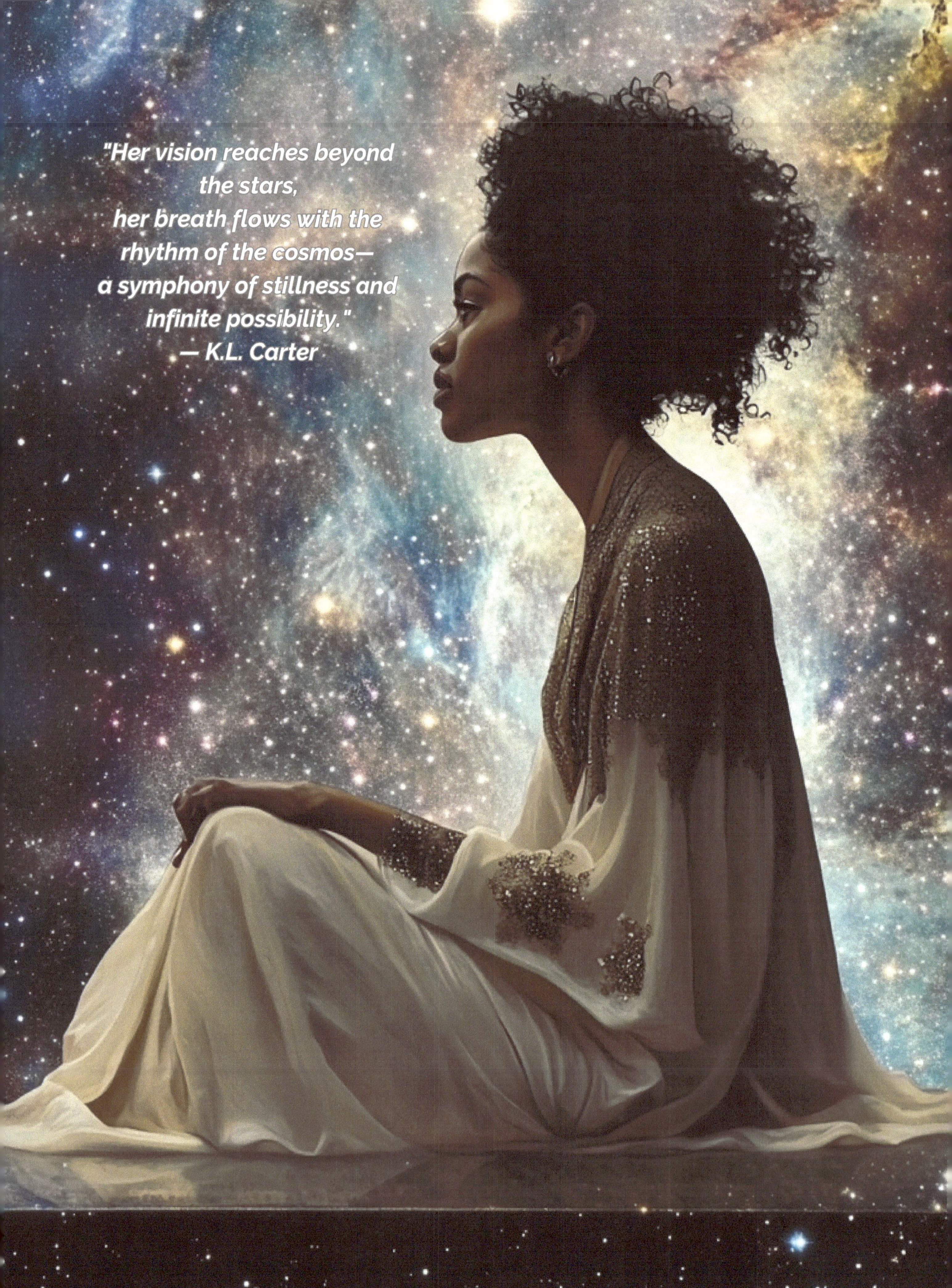
"Her vision reaches beyond
the stars,
her breath flows with the
rhythm of the cosmos—
a symphony of stillness and
infinite possibility."
— K.L. Carter

Author's Note
K. L. Carter

"Mystical Girl, the stars have always known your name. Your journey leads not outward, but inward to the brilliance within—a limitless self, radiant and whole."
— K.L. Carter

Dear Reader,

This book is a journey—a reflection of the stars above and the universe within. It is an ode to the Mystical Girl in all of us, that part of our soul seeking to explore, to discover, and to grow.

As someone who has spent a career immersed in the wonders of space exploration, I've come to realize that the most profound journeys are not always measured in miles or light-years, but in moments of self-discovery. The same curiosity that drives us to explore the cosmos also propels us inward, to the vast landscapes of our inner worlds.

This book was born out of that duality: the balance of reaching outward to the stars and inward to our souls. It reflects my belief that we are each a constellation of infinite possibilities, capable of extraordinary growth, creativity, and joy.

Thank you for allowing me to share this journey with you. I hope these pages inspire you to pause, reflect, and embrace the wonder that is uniquely yours.

With gratitude and starlight,

K.L. Carter

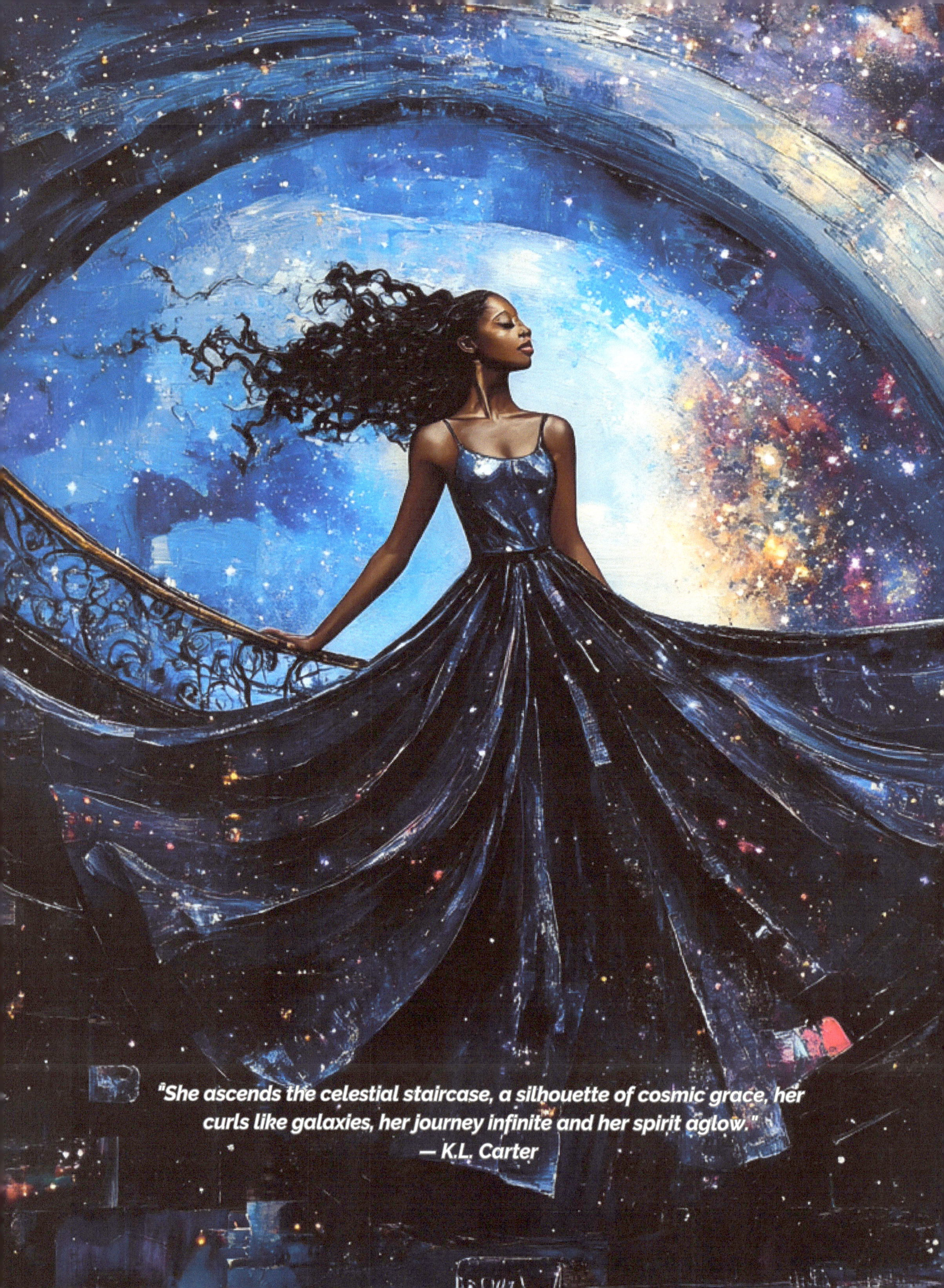
"She ascends the celestial staircase, a silhouette of cosmic grace, her
curls like galaxies, her journey infinite and her spirit aglow."
— K.L. Carter

About the Author
K. L. Carter

"The univer*se is vast, but so is the space within you."*
— K.L. Carter

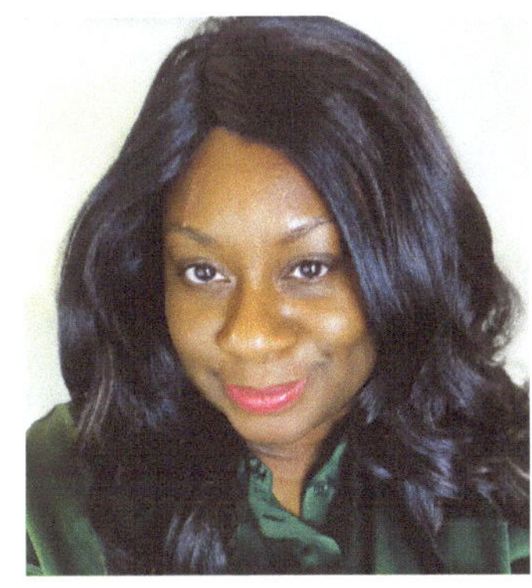

K.L. Carter is a physicist, aerospace professional, and lifelong dreamer captivated by the mysteries of the universe. With a career spanning the NASA Space Shuttle Program, the International Space Station (ISS), commercial space exploration, and the next generation of space technology, she has spent her life exploring both the cosmos and the depths of human potential.

Her passion for empowering others is reflected in her writing, blending themes of mindfulness, self-discovery, and cosmic wonder. Through her work, she encourages readers to explore their own journeys with curiosity, courage, and an open heart.

When she's not gazing at the stars, chasing the moon, or writing about personal transformation, K.L. Carter enjoys inspiring others through mentorship, reflecting on life's big questions, and spending time with her family. Her love for the cosmos is rivaled only by her belief in the boundless potential within each of us.

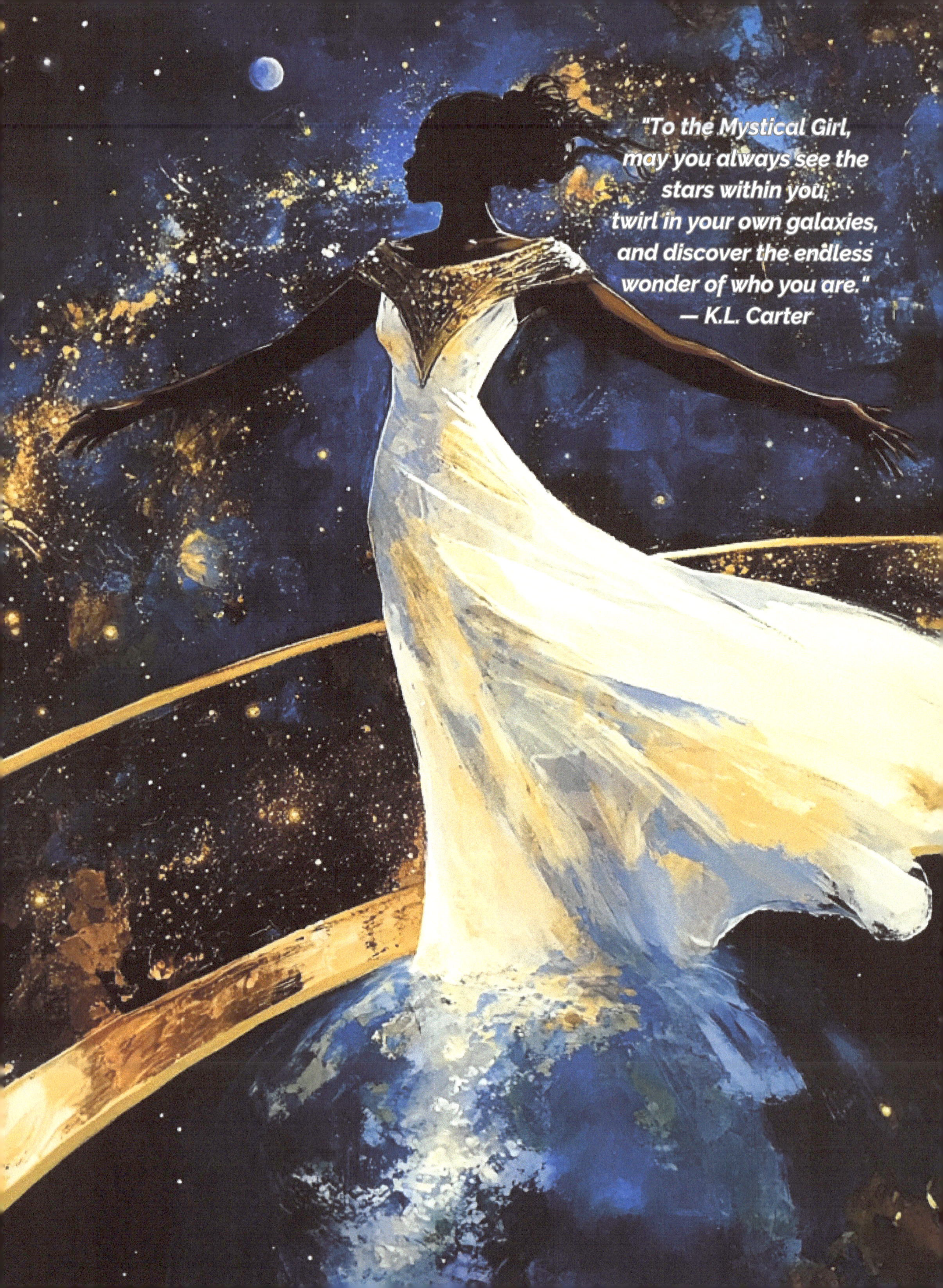
"To the Mystical Girl,
may you always see the
stars within you,
twirl in your own galaxies,
and discover the endless
wonder of who you are."
— K.L. Carter

www.ingramcontent.com/pod-product-compliance
Lightning Source LLC
LaVergne TN
LVHW070222110826
845147LV00003B/622

9798992278026